Ladybugs

Aaron Frisch

CREATIVE EDUCATION

seedlings

Published by Creative Education
P.O. Box 227, Mankato, Minnesota 56002
Creative Education is an imprint of
The Creative Company
www.thecreativecompany.us

Design and production by Ellen Huber
Art direction by Rita Marshall
Printed in the United States of America

Photographs by 123rf (Ivan Mikhaylov), Bigstock (mbridger),
Biosphoto (Samuel Dhier), Dreamstime (Alexstar, Ivan
Mikhaylov, Morskaya20031), iStockphoto (Kerstin Klaassen,
Laurie Knight, Collin Lim, Tomasz Pietryszek), Shutterstock
(AdStock RF, Potapov Alexander, Arsgera, Alin Brotea,
Elnur, irin-k, Liew Weng Keong, Henrik Larsson, Ad Oculos,
South12th Photography, SweetCrisis), SuperStock (NHPA),
Veer (irin-k, Pakhnyushchyy Vitaliy)

Library of Congress Cataloging-in-Publication Data
Frisch, Aaron.
Ladybugs / Aaron Frisch.
p. cm. — (Seedlings)
Includes bibliographical references and index.
Summary: A kindergarten-level introduction to ladybugs,
covering their growth process, behaviors, the places they call
home, and such defining physical features as their spotted
shells.
ISBN 978-1-60818-459-0
1. Ladybugs—Juvenile literature. I. Title.

QL596.C65F75 2014
595.76'9—dc23   2013029070

CCSS: RI.K.1, 2, 3, 4, 5, 6, 7;
RI.1.1, 2, 3, 4, 5, 6, 7; RF.K.1, 3; RF.1.1

First Edition
9 8 7 6 5 4 3 2 1

TABLE OF CONTENTS

Hello, ladybugs!

Ladybugs are bugs
that fly. Ladybugs
live in many places.

Sometimes they get into people's houses!

Ladybugs have round shells.

The shells have black or white spots.

A ladybug's shell covers its wings.

The wings come out when the ladybug flies.

Ladybugs eat mites and aphids. Some kinds of ladybugs eat plants.

Baby ladybugs come from eggs.

They look like worms with legs.
Then they grow shells.

Ladybugs try to find mates. They fly around.

Goodbye, ladybugs!

Picture a Ladybug

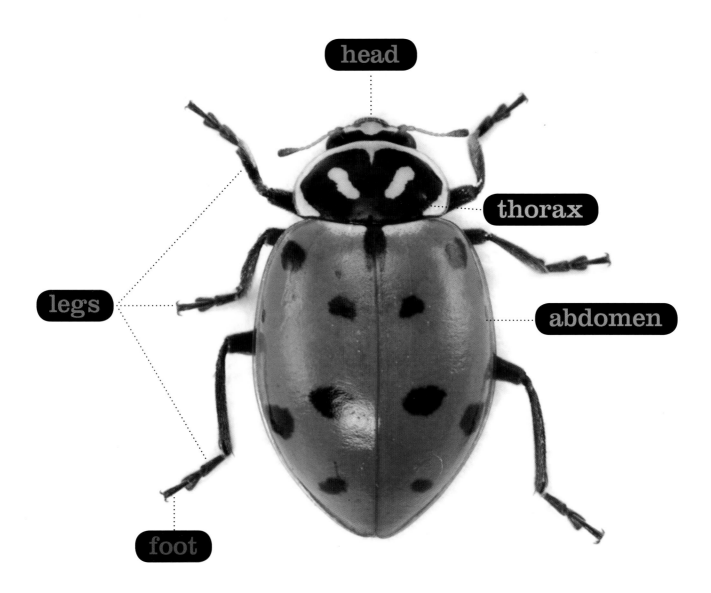

head

thorax

legs

abdomen

foot

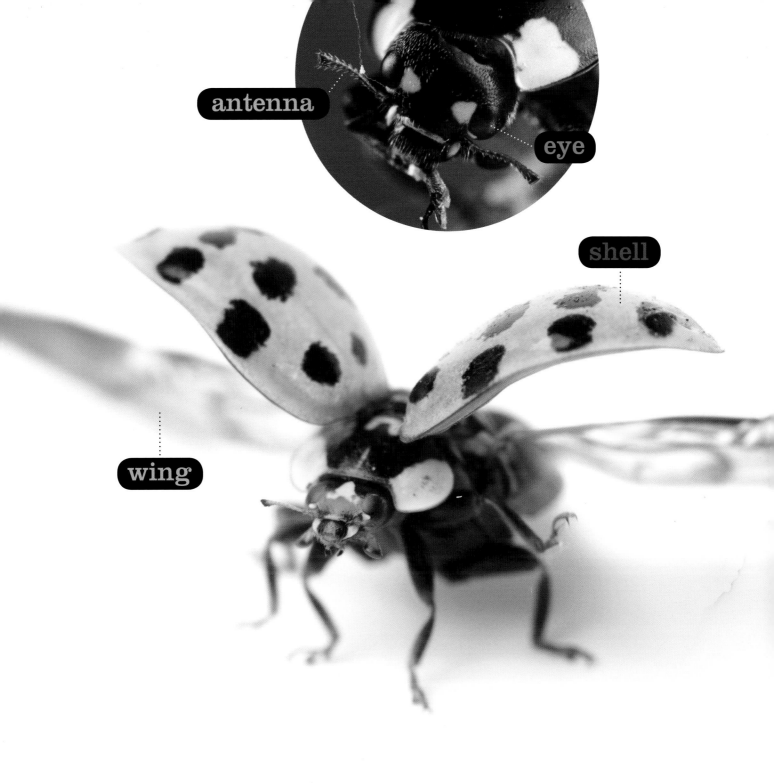

antenna

eye

shell

wing

Words to Know

aphids: bugs with soft bodies that live on plants

mates: other animals to have babies with

mites: tiny animals with eight legs that live on plants or in dirt

shells: hard coverings

Read More

Allen, Judy. *Are You a Ladybug?*
New York: Kingfisher, 2000.

Rustad, Martha E. H. *Ladybugs*.
Minneapolis: Bellwether Media, 2008.

Websites

DLTK's Crafts for Kids: Ladybug Activities
http://www.dltk-kids.com/crafts/insects/crafts-ladybug.htm
Choose a ladybug craft to do. Or print and color ladybug
pictures.

Ladybug Jigsaw Puzzle
http://www.first-school.ws/puzzlesonline/animals/ladybug.htm
Put together a puzzle with a picture of a ladybug.

Index